Monday Motivation
By Anthony Chiles

Sign up for the author's newsletter to learn about new releases. To sign up, visit: www.anthonychiles.com

CONTENTS

INTRODUCTION

Monday Motivation is a collection of fifty-two motivational essays. The book is designed to be simple and inspiring. These motivations are not just for Mondays, but for whenever they are needed. Read one per week, sit down and read it all at once, or flip through until you see one that calls to you. How you consume the book does not matter. What matters is that the words motivate you to be your very best.

On each title page is a photo taken by me. The images tell the story of the last days of my office job in Columbus, Ohio, my solo drive across the country to Los Angeles, and the sites in this city that have inspired me since relocating here.

When I first made the choice to walk away from the career I had dedicated ten years of my life to, I had many conversations with myself. I questioned my plan, my rationale, and my sanity. I wrote many of the words in this book as a way to motivate myself through that difficult decision-making process. When I began to share these words with others, I realized I was not the only one in need of motivation to get through the week. Many friends appreciated the words I was sharing through social media, so I took the ideas that resonated with me the most and compiled them into this collection to help readers find that motivational boost they need at any time. I wish you well in whatever you decide to do with your life, and I hope my words can help you on the journey.

~Anthony Chiles

CONSUME LESS

1

In the midst of consumption, you can lose who you are in what you possess. Having more means having more responsibility. The things you purchase need to be maintained, insured, and safely stored when you're away. This requires time, energy, and money. If you aren't careful, what you own will end up controlling you. The freedom to follow your passion can be stifled by looming debt and the responsibility of "stuff." Things do not make you happy. Your job title, your bank accounts, and your cars do not define you. What does define you is how you treat others, and what you do for those closest to you. Once you secure your basic needs, your priority should be to serve the needs of others and not consume more goods than you need. Your time would be well spent building relationships. Don't allow yourself to fall victim to the myth that you can buy happiness. Instead, accept the truth that serving others and being generous will last longer and bring more joy than any "thing" you can ever own.

Do what you love. Don't ignore your internal voice for the noise of friends, family, and society. Their intentions may be good, and their opinions should be respected, but if you completely ignore yourself, you may end up feeling stuck in a place you do not belong. To get to a place of consistent happiness, you have to pursue your passion without concern of the judgment of others. You don't have to take the road most traveled. You don't have to be afraid of failure. Believe that doing what you love is a realistic and achievable goal. Decide to break free from what holds you back from the life you want to live. This is your life, so live your life exceptionally. Live it doing what you love and loving what you do.

You were created for something. Your purpose is the reason you're here. It's that thing that you were meant to do. It may take years of experimenting and working to discover that purpose, or it may be the passion that you've had since childhood. No matter how long it takes to find that purpose. . . find it! Then work on that purpose with all of your potential. Potential is what you are capable of doing. The purpose of a pen is to write, while the potential of a pen is to write the greatest story ever. Potential is revealed by how hard you work. Potential does not need to be in line with purpose. Your potential, which can be revealed in different avenues, is how far you could go. The key is to unleash full potential while operating in your purpose. That's when life becomes great!

You have specific talents that you naturally want to share with the world. You wanted to share these talents so much that they came flowing out as soon as you were able to communicate them to the world. As a child, you sang and danced. You were a painter, a sculptor, and an actor. You wrote, you built, you played, and you thrived. Then you learned that you weren't as good as other singers, so you stopped singing. You learned that there was no money in drawing or painting or playing, so you stopped that too. Eventually, you stopped sharing many of your talents, believing that you weren't good enough. But you have the courage to share all of yourself, and you've had it ever since you were a child. Find that courage, discover those latent talents, and begin to give what you were meant to give. Whether you use your talents to affect millions or simply bring a smile to one person's face, you can make the world a better place, and that's something worth sharing.

DON'T JUST
"JOB"

A job is different than work. Work is an activity involving mental or physical effort done in order to achieve a purpose or result. A job is doing work to earn money. You were more than likely led to believe that money is the ruler used to measure your success. And more than likely, you have *jobbed* hard for many hours and for someone else's purpose, with little regard for how the work you're doing will further your own purpose. Working then becomes associated with jobbing. In reality, not working toward your own dream or purpose becomes an unfulfilling endeavor. Be a dream worker, not a wage worker. Of course, rent can't be paid in dreams, but that does not mean your life has to be completely absent of working toward your dreams. Decide to live for your purpose instead of a paycheck. Make this choice, and you'll find yourself heading in the direction of peace, fulfillment, happiness, and abundant living.

Your focus is a powerful tool. Your ability to set your focus on a single thought for a prolonged period of time is the key to everything you want in life. Thoughts are ephemeral. Every day, thousands of thoughts will enter into your mind and vanish as quickly as they've come. The thoughts you choose to grab hold of and focus on will define what you do with your time and energy. The longer you focus on an idea, the more it will influence your creativity, imagination, and actions. Also, no goal can be accomplished without focus, because focus is the key to completing tasks and getting things done. But a word of caution: the incredible power of focus has the potential to be extremely destructive. If you focus on the *wrong* thoughts, the ones that are demeaning, self-sabotaging and abusive, then those thoughts will define you. Use your focus wisely, and it will transform your life.

BE
CONSISTENT

The difference between those who achieve their dreams and goals and those who do not is largely determined by behavior. You have to decide to take actions that get you closer to your dream each and every hour of each and every day. You have to decide to be your best and consistently repeat your best as you move closer to achieving your goal. Remind yourself why you are doing what you do. Then do it. Then, do it again the next day, and the next day, and the day after that, because you are what you do. That's what defines you. That's what identifies you. Doing things consistently builds trust. That trust comes because the people around you know, from one day to the next that your actions can be relied on. They will take risks with you because they feel safe that who you are is who you will continue to be. And when this trust is built, people will go out of their way to grant you with (or recommend you for) opportunities. But you have to be consistent.

STAY
PREPARED

Opportunities to do what you want to do with your time and talent are presented to people every day. New opportunities are being developed and refined everyday. In order to take advantage of those opportunities, you must be in a position to both know about them and capitalize on them. You must be prepared. No matter what work you choose to do, learn and master your craft. Work on your craft daily so that your skills never diminish. Learn new skills so that you can add value to your life and your relationships. Keep your eyes and ears on the industry you work in so you stay informed. Life will not typically give you much prep time. When a job or position presents itself, the people offering that position are not going to wait for you to "eventually" get ready. But if you stay ready, you will always be prepared. Preparedness can be the difference between your dream opportunity going to you or to the next person. Prepare yourself.

Your mind is a fascinating, complex command center that generations of doctors and scientist across the globe have spent their entire lives trying to understand, only to discover that more and more mysteries are still hidden deep inside. Utilizing the mind effectively is the most powerful tool and the most valuable resource you have. Thinking optimistic thoughts can positively affect the way you feel, the way you address problems, and the way you project yourself to the world. Thinking about ideas and possibilities can create businesses or art or inventions that can have an influence on humanity. You cannot expect to be who you want to be and achieve the success in life you want by thinking about things that break you down, create fear and doubt, or distract you from your goal. Everything you want in life begins with you thinking that you can have it. Every invention, government, and creative work started as a thought. Find whatever is true, whatever inspires, whatever motivates, whatever is lovely, whatever is admirable. Find things that are excellent or praiseworthy, and think about those things. Your optimist thoughts will change your world.

When you determine you want something in life, you must decide firmly on a course of action and then move forward with your chosen course of action. Your motivation to achieve what you want can drown in the ocean of responsibilities from work, family, relationships, and the unexpected stress of life. When facing what seems like an overload of responsibility, many people lose focus on their aspirations. They forget about their goals and operate by being responsive to the obstacles. Instead resolve to spend time each day engaging in activities that will bring you closer to what you desire. Be determined to do better and act better in order to get what you want. Live a life where you decide, then do, without excuse or distraction. To resolve requires action, which differs from just desiring something. It is not enough to want better or to want more or to simply dream. Everybody has desire. What you need to obtain what you desire is not *more* desire. What you need is resolve.

Pursuit is an action word. A pursuit is a chase, a hunt, or a quest; something requiring effort and energy. The famous statement "pursuit of Happiness" informs you that happiness does not come easily. You have to go after it, seize it, and try your best to hold on to that which brings you happiness. No rule or law can ensure happiness. No amount of money, great or small, can ensure happiness. No relationship, no title, and no amount of fame automatically brings you happiness. Happiness must be pursued. The pursuit of happiness is an ever-changing, yet ever-constant internal quest that you will endure. The pursuit of happiness will often be difficult. Knowing the difficulty of seeking uncommon joy keeps some people from going after it. They would much rather live in a comfortable situation while being miserable than step outside of their comfort zone to seek happiness. If you're doing things with the sole purpose of living comfortably, with no regard to how happy you are, reevaluate your situation and your values. Do the things you want to do in order to live happily.

PUT IN WORK

If you want something you have to work for it. Nothing is created without some form of energy being transferred. Working hard means transferring the mental and physical energy from your body into the process or system that will yield the results you desire. With that said, there is something extremely important to remember: you will not get everything you work for. There will be times when you put a lot of energy and focus on a particular goal and never reach it. Failure is a possibility. As discouraging as failure may sound, it's not as bad as regret, and regret is the only thing you are left with if you do not give your best effort toward accomplishing the goals you set. Although you may not always get what you work for, you will certainly have to work for what you do get. There is no secret to success, because it's not a secret: you have to work for it.

What you *do* matters most. You have your beliefs. You have your opinions. Your environment, culture, and social interactions have shaped your world view since birth. As a social being, naturally you want to talk about how you feel and what you think about the world around you. The thing to be mindful of is that too much talking doesn't leave much time for getting things done. Your words are extremely powerful, yet they can never match the power of your actions. If you wake up every morning for a year and say, "I will go for a run this morning," it will never have the health benefits of waking up and actually going on that daily run. Intending to create something will never mean as much as actually creating it. The smallest deeds trump the greatest of intentions every time, and those deeds define you.

YOU ARE
CLOSE

You're closer than you think to living the life you want to live! But it can be difficult to spend so much time and energy on a particular goal, and *then* be told that even more time and energy needs to be expended to reach it. Your frustration, anxiety, and fears are all justified, but if you shift your thinking, you can eliminate those negative emotions. For your dreams to manifest they only require you to do one thing at a time. So for today, focus on creating one piece, and tomorrow focus on the next piece, and day by day, you will create the whole. Don't dwell on how high the mountain is, just focus on the next step. Think about how close you are to the next step, and trust that the process will get you to your final destination.

BE HAPPY

You have probably said to yourself, "I will be happy when _____ happens." Or maybe you have said, "I will have happiness when I have _____." It would serve you best to simply think, "I will be happy now." Then, take appropriate actions in order to achieve your specific dreams and goals and avoid attaching your happiness to future events. Attaching your happiness to a future event is sabotaging your happiness every day. In the same way the horizon lies in the distance, no matter how far or how fast you travel, your happiness will forever be in the distance. Tell yourself "I will be happy now." Determine to be happy. Then decide what will make your life happy. When you decide to find joy in any circumstance, you will find that you can be happy now *and* be happy later.

BE CONFIDENT

Walking across the room was, at one time, the most difficult thing you ever did. The skills of balancing and coordinating your legs and body once seemed impossible. Then, after many falls and stumbles and much practice, walking became easy. You learned to walk boldly without fear, doubt, or stress. You learned to walk with confidence. Once you mastered the skills needed for walking, you gained confidence to master other more challenging skills. Each victory positioned you for the next level of progress. From walking, to running, from running to playing sports, the mastery of a skill set is the foundation of growth. The reason people can dive out of airplanes, rush into battlefields, and run into burning buildings with confidence is because they have mastered the skill set necessary to thrive in those situations. A lack of confidence often can be traced back to fear due to a lack of skill. Do not be afraid. You have the capacity for confidence and you have had it ever since you attempted your first steps. No matter what you choose to do, master the skills necessary to do it so you can do it with confidence.

Freedom can exist even when the body is bound, and bondage can exist even when the body is free. The slaves in American history that wrote hymns and kept their hope knew that slavery didn't happen by locking the body, because slavery happens by locking the mind and removing dreams. If you're not careful, you can become a slave to your fear, your history, or your beliefs. You may not even be aware that you are not free. With all the chaos that exists in the world, restricting your mind from all of the beauty is easy. But even in the midst of violence, rage, genocide, wars, and other atrocities, you can still find a way to let your mind be free to dream, have faith, hope, and love. Learn from the American ancestors who lived in chains and struggled through life but never gave up their minds. Keep your mind unlocked and never give up your dreams.

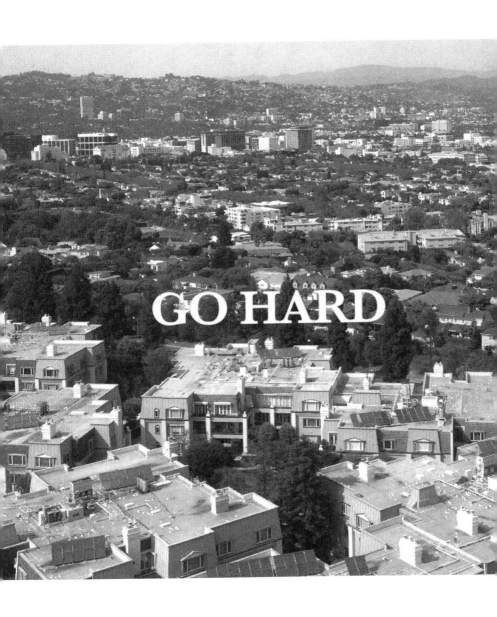

GO HARD

When you decide to do something, go hard! Don't hold back. Whatever you do, do it with all of your might. Commit to your decisions and own the results, regardless of whether they are the results you expected or not. Going halfway will only leave room for excuses or regrets. Be all-in. There is comfort in doing things with only a fraction of your effort, because then, if you fail, you can justify the failure by saying you didn't try as hard as you could have. But comfort is not the friend to success. Just give everything you can reasonably give, day after day, month after month, and year after year. In your relationships, your work, and your play, go hard. Never let the people around you think of mediocrity or laziness when they think of you. Be wise in your efforts. Do not overexert yourself or neglect responsibility for the attainment of a different goal, but be willing to do the most with the time you have. Just go for it and go hard!

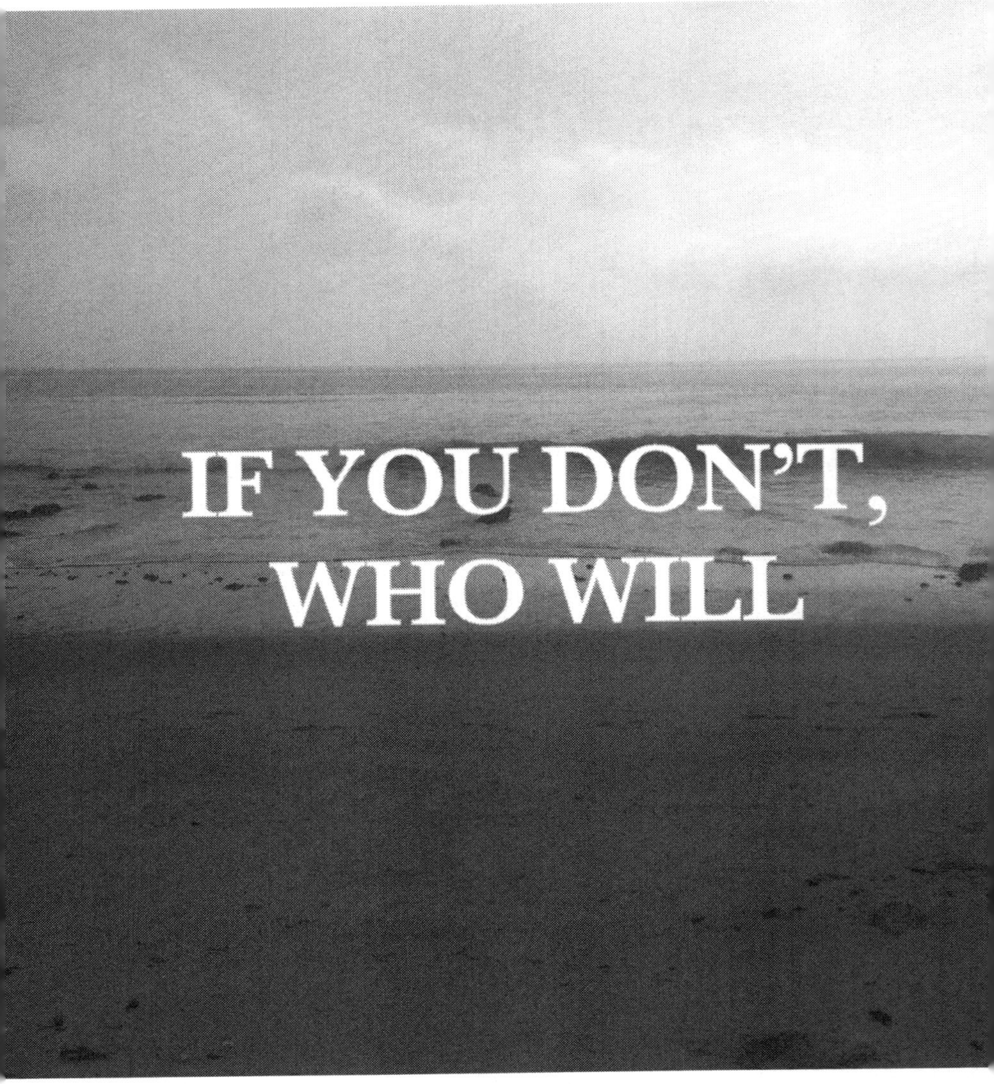
IF YOU DON'T,
WHO WILL

If you don't, who will? No one else has your imagination. No one else has your unique combination of experiences, intelligence, and passion. You are unique and wonderful and purpose-filled. If you don't fulfill that purpose, who will? In the history of the universe, and in the entire future of the universe, there will be only one of you. The time you live, the body you have, the genes that construct your cells, the mind you possess, and the environment you were shaped by is a one-time occurrence on a cosmic timeline. You have to embrace the awesomeness of that reality. You have to live in the greatness that is your miraculous existence. And you have to believe that if you don't create the things that are in your soul to create, then nobody else can. They certainly can't do it the way you can with your own unique abilities. Be the lover you always imagined you could be, be the parent you always envisioned, or be the sibling or friend you always wanted in your life. Be the best you. Know yourself, give the world the best of yourself, and believe that if you don't pour your essence out into the world, no one else will.

CONTROL
YOUR MIND

You possess one of the most powerful tools in the entire known Universe: the human mind. Your mind is an instrument that took billions of years to create. You can comprehend the smallest subatomic particle, the entire universe, and even beyond. Your mind is able to imagine things unseen and create processes to make the unreal, real. And your sole focus should be to develop the discipline to take complete control of your mind. Controlling your mind will be the key to unlocking all that you want because making the choice to do something grants you unspeakable power. So much in life may be considered "out of control," but your mental attitude is always within your control. Take full control of it! You must embrace the focus and concentration required to gain the full awareness of your mind and where it may take you.

PREPARE
YOURSELF

If you are like most people, you prepare for the "big day." The interview for the dream job, the day you pop the question, the big game, that encounter with a long-lost loved one. You get ready when the big stuff comes. You make sure you have your outfit in order, and you go over what you are going to do and say, (rehearsing and revising and rehearsing some more). You get ready. But when you have a grand vision, a huge goal or a great dream, it isn't enough to get ready when the time comes. Instead, you have to stay ready. Preparation can't be an occasional activity. Preparation has to be a daily habit. Even if nothing appears to be coming your way, you have to sharpen your skills. You have to hone your craft. You have to understand that, at any moment, the opportunity to make that dream a reality could be presented to you. So, prepare yourself because if you stay ready, you won't have to get ready.

SHOW, DON'T TELL

The ability to execute a plan will make the difference between obtaining what you propose to have in life, and simply talking about what you want to have. Because we all enjoy a good story, we often enjoy creating the story of what our lives could be, or what we plan to do with our lives once this or that happens. The problem with telling stories is that the act of saying what you would like to have happen in the future will do little toward actually making it happen. Yes, it is necessary for you to generate some publicity in order to find those willing to invest in your dreams, but way more time should be spent working than spent talking about your work. We live in an era where individuals would rather spend time on how they are perceived than invest the time to master their craft. Just get the work done. Don't submit to the desire to brag. Stop telling people what you are going to do and begin doing.

LIVE BEYOND
THE TANGIBLE

Who you are goes beyond the material world. What you know and observe about the world around you is only a fraction of what is there. You aren't your clothes, car, house, bank account, or even your body. Embrace this idea so that you don't consume all your time and energy pursuing things that are insubstantial. The things that matter most are not measurable in amount. The things that matter most are the quality of the bonds you create with the people and the world around you, because everything in the universe is connected. What gives life meaning is the love you give and receive. Walk in constant awareness of this knowledge. Value connection over stuff. Value relationships over material goods. Create experiences that bring you joy and bring joy to the people around you. The memories you create and share with others can't be bottled up or sold, but they are your most valuable possession. Make more of those memories. Don't invest everything in the tangible world where material goods can be here today and gone tomorrow. Invest in the relationship you have with the Creator and all that's been created.

ADJUST YOUR FOCUS

If you live long enough, you discover that "life happens." Joy and sadness happen. Love and pain happen. Frustration, weariness, and loss exist alongside accomplishment, excitement, and celebration. This is life, and when life happens, accessing how you feel about the circumstances life has presented is only natural. But the more you shift your focus from self, the more peace you'll find. The less value you place on both success and failure, the more calm exists in your life. The highs and the lows and the ebb and flow begin to minimize when you are less self-centered and more humanity-centered. Like a guitar string pulled just right, your life becomes tuned when you focus on the world around you and not on the world inside you. Because you are part of this world, be aware of how you feel, what you sense, and what your state of being is. But do not allow that to overshadow the value in being aware of the people and the world around you.

TEAMS WORK

Humans are made to collaborate. You are genetically encoded to be a social being. The longing you have to connect with other humans has existed from your date of birth. In your infancy, you depended on people for your most basic needs of food and water, as well as your more complex needs of love and acceptance. As you aged, you became less dependent on others, but you never become fully independent of others. It has been written that no one is an island, and you are no exception. This is especially true when you desire to accomplish big goals. Going after something as complex as your dream without connecting and working with others would be foolish. You need the generosity and talents of others. You need your squad, team, tribe, or crew. It doesn't matter how you define it, but it is important that you surround yourself with like-minded individuals of different expertise in order to accomplish your goals. Cooperation makes even the impossible doable. Don't try to achieve it alone. A task worth completing, a dream worth pursuing, and a life worth living will require many helping hands along the way.

PLAN YOUR WORK

Everything begins as an idea. The first step in turning a dream into a reality is to constantly hold your vision of the future in your mind. You must know without an ounce of doubt that you belong in the amazing circumstances you envision. Once that affirmation is secure in your mind, the work begins. You live in a universe made of energy, so you have to put out energy to convert your grand vision into reality. Create a series of small goals, each of which will get you closer to your desire. Give yourself a measurable task to complete on a weekly basis. Set dates to get your task done. Hold yourself accountable for your failures and celebrate your successes. When you have been given a vision, you have been given a seed, and though it's fun to imagine how great life will be once that seed is fully grown, that seed is still just a seed until you do the work. Plan your work, work your plan, and be patient as your vision manifest into reality.

KNOW YOUR
OBJECTIVE

Actors have an objective for each scene they are in, and each choice they make should move them toward achieving that objective. Once an actor establishes an objective, the physical actions of their body, the tone of their voice, the rate they speak the words, and their internal thoughts all focus on obtaining that objective. You have the lead role in your life, so you have to find your own objective. A life of abundance and wellness requires that you discover and establish your definite chief aim. Once you determine that objective, make sure that each and every choice is in line with it. Every day you have to decide what you are going to do to get closer to your end goal. Judge every action based on how close it will get you to your objective. The clothes you wear, the food you eat, and the people you interact with should all be in line with your purpose. Think, choose, and act with your objective in mind. Let your objective be your primary focus on the *stage* of your life.

WHY DO YOU DO WHAT YOU DO

What is your *why*? Your *why* is the reason you do the things you do. Your *why* is as distinctly yours as your personality is. For some it's for a friend or family member. For some it's for their country, for humanity, for legacy, or for God. But the person, place, or thing that drives you has to be constantly present. The reason why you do the things you do has to be front and center in your mind so that every decision, every hour of every day is in line with your *why*. You have to have a clear reason to do what you do. It's not enough to just want *something*. It's not even enough to have the good fortune of achieving something grand. The difference between being fulfilled in your doing, instead of just doing things for the sake of doing them, is being able to wake up everyday with a distinct and potent reason for your actions.

SEE THE WORLD
WITH JOY

If you change the lenses you look through to see the world, then you change the way your world looks. Once you decide to embrace a positive outlook, it influences your relationships, work, habits, and character. Being happy and optimistic is not about ignoring problems, but expanding your view and opening your mind to see the solutions to the problems. A happy world view doesn't mean you pretend that the negative doesn't exist; it means that you allow your mind to be grateful for the positive that does exist as well as searching for ways to transform the negative into a positive. It is both measurable and quantifiable that the human brain, when operating in a relaxed and positive state, is more alert, focused, better at problem solving, and more efficient. Seeing the world through the lens of happiness will make your life and the lives of those around you better.

KNOW WHAT
YOU WANT

It's very important to know what you want. In order to make your goal or dream a reality, you should first define what it is that you want as clearly and as specifically as possible. Also, educate yourself about what it is that you want. You may see or hear something that sparks your interest or ignites your passion and then decide to pursue that person or thing. But taking the time to learn more about what you want can save you from lost time or energy you can easily spend on something that was different than you imagined it to be. The fantasy is often more exciting than the reality. Learn the reality of a situation by talking to people who know the person you want to connect with, have been to the place you want to visit, or have done the thing you want to do. Using patience and wisdom before diving in headfirst could save you many headaches and much heartache.

It's simple. If you want something you have to work for it. Nothing is created without a seed, and seeds do not grow without taking in a lot of energy. Just as actual plant seeds in the earth need the energy from the sun to produce fruit, your idea "seeds" require energy in order to produce what you want. And you might not get everything you work for. Some spend their entire lives working toward outcomes they never achieve. This is life. Yet one thing is certain--without putting in the work, you cannot realistically expect to get what you want. Constantly keep your hand to the plow. You never know which one of your gifts will generate the greatest return, so make the most of your time and work at your talents until you've mastered them. Successful people have two common characteristics. One is that they all have multiple and varied projects and do not allow their hands to be idle. Two, they work hard!

The courage it takes to follow your heart and pursue your dream, the thing you'll always love doing, is hard to find. It's rare to find people who are living the life they dreamed about living. Most people don't do what it is they are most passionate about. But you are not most people; you are brave. Everything you need is already inside of you. The passion and intelligence is already there. You are enough. Embrace the reality that you are enough. You are smart enough, capable enough, and courageous enough to make the leap into the next big thing in your life. Having courage won't eliminate obstacles or take away from the struggles you will inevitably face. Courage means facing the fears, temptations, obstacles, and pain with strength. You can do it. You are brave. Believe it.

BE YOUR BEST

Be great at what you do! Don't settle for anything less than the best you can give of yourself. People hold back because they don't want to give too much. The world has more than enough people doing less than their best because they "don't feel like it," because they have decided what they want is not worth the time, energy and effort, or because they feel entitled to receive what they want without the work. You need to be the exception to the rule. Take the attention off of yourself. Put that attention on what you are doing and the people you are doing it for. Do amazing work. Understand that your best will change from one day to the next. Your physical, mental, and emotional state will have an impact on what your best looks like, but never make excuses as to why you are not being the best you can possibly be. Give the world and yourself your best each day, and you will be amazed at what you will receive in return. If you sow your best, you will reap the best.

You are valuable and the world needs to know it. Do not be afraid of marketing yourself. Let the world see what you are offering. Show how you add value to society. The platforms available to showcase your ideas, talents, and creations are vast and continue to expand. Hop aboard those platforms and proudly showcase the work that you do. You can be brilliant and broke if you refuse to take the time to promote yourself. Don't hide your skills and abilities out of fear or laziness. The talents that you have stewardship over are not meant to be buried away--they are meant to have a positive impact on the world. And the world will never feel that impact if you do not speak up. Take to the streets and the Internet and showcase what you do. Be wise in what you share and come from a place of giving, not wanting attention or praise. Be humble, yet unapologetic, in your expressions. Let your light shine!

PUSH THROUGH
THE FEAR

Proceed, even when you are afraid. Sometimes the giants in your life are really titans, even bigger and scarier than you imagined. It may be that the odds are stacked against you. Don't let that stop you. You may feel like you can't make it through, but you can. Just keep going. Keep moving forward. There is no such thing as doing nothing, so allowing fear to paralyze you only means you have the engine running, but you aren't moving forward. Go forward. No matter what happens, you will gain a valuable life experience. Your greatest success will come from your greatest sacrifice, and you will learn most from your greatest failures. You will face obstacles and resistance but push through. You'll be stronger on the other side.

A NO IS NOT
THE END

You are only one *yes* away from being on hold to moving forward, and every no gets you closer to that *yes*. Rejection is an inevitable part of the process of moving from one place in life to another. People will tell you no because they don't have the ability or willingness to assist you at that time. Those no's only get you closer to your *yes*. Don't be discouraged by them. Accept them for what they are, a declaration by one person who is not on the same page as you. A rejection is not a declaration of your worth. It does not define who you are or what you are capable of. And even if you hear no a thousand times, it only helps to eliminate the clutter en route to your yes. Rejection is not the end--only the beginning to a new possibility.

GO WHERE
YOU THRIVE

Don't settle for comfort in a "good job" with a "good company." If you're not in your right environment, you will never reach your full potential. You may survive, but you will not experience the greatness that exists within you until you find that sweet spot of doing what you are meant to do and being where you are meant to be. A shark is ruthless in the ocean but helpless in the desert. Go where you thrive. You need to know yourself, know the environment that best serves you, and then do your best to get there. Being where you're supposed to be doesn't mean you have to leave your town. If that's where you're meant to be, the people and resources you need to thrive will be there. Sometimes you do have to leave. If you have to leave, be willing to leave. If you are willing but unable to move, use your imagination to think about ways to gather the resources to make the move happen. If you are not willing, know that there is nothing to fear. Get free from the bonds of comfort and be where you're supposed to be in order to thrive.

Your daily routine will determine your future. Your habits will make or break you. Your life is a series of actions from the time you wake up until you decide to go to bed. If you are disciplined in your behavior, your quality of life will reflect that discipline. Your abilities may not be identical or equal to someone else, but you do have equal time in a day. Make the most of that time. Use that time efficiently through disciplined behavior. Discipline is the key to unlocking your potential, so manage your life's tasks. Know where your time is being invested and how well your investments are paying off. Be intentional with even the most casual of activities. From brushing your teeth, to talking on the phone, to scrolling through social media, do things with purpose. The summation of the choices you've made before define who you were, not who you can become if you live a disciplined life.

BE A SERVANT

When you shift from self-focus and self-interest and move to the mindset of serving others, your life, and ultimately the world, becomes better. Ask what you can give, rather than what you can get. Be a servant and carry that title with pride. That doesn't mean dismissing your own ambition blindly to follow the mission someone else has in life. It does mean that you have to accept that the passion you have was placed inside of you for a reason, and that reason is to serve humanity. A servant performs duties for others. A servant is attentive to the needs of others. A servant is a devoted helper. All of these qualities can exist regardless of your profession. Whether you're an artist, engineer, parent, CEO, or waiter, you can serve others. So, be a servant and be proud of it.

THE WORLD
NEEDS YOU

The world needs you. In you lies a secret that no one else can ever know or share. That secret is your hidden potential. Your potential is the summation of all the experiences, environments, nurture and nature that make you who you are. Only you can reveal yourself to the world, and the world needs the best you that you can be. Let no day go by without getting the most out of it. Do as much as you can do. Learn as much as you can learn. See as much as you can see. And most importantly, give as much as you can give. Create and share because someone's life will be made better because of you. The world needs you. Its greatest resource is people, and you are immeasurably valuable. Please, let no one, including yourself, convince you of anything other than the fact that you are amazing, because you are. Embrace your wonder, accept your awesomeness, and go do the things that bring you joy and make the world a better place. The world needs you.

GIVE

Your measure of success should not be how much you can acquire in the world, but how much you can give. The rich may become famous, but the givers become legends. The men and women who sacrifice their time, energy, and effort for the well being of others are never forgotten. This includes serving your family and your neighborhood. You may not have a national holiday in your honor, but you will live on in the hearts and minds of those around you, and they will share your story to the generations that come afterward. It's not how much you can take, but how much you can give. It's not how much you can acquire, but how much you can contribute. Stars that exploded billions of years ago gave the universe the material that makes up cells in your body. Guardians in your home and outside your home gave of their time and energy to keep you warm, secure, and fed as a child so that you could grow. You have been given a tremendous amount from the universe and from other people just to be alive in this moment. Give your best because so much was given to you.

STRIVE FOR GREATNESS

Your sole responsibility in life is to bring your very best--every day, every time--in everything you do. How can some athletes set a world record and then break the world record they set? Because those who are great at what they do don't compare themselves to those around them. Instead they ask themselves, "Is this the best I can do?" The greats do things that the majority of people refuse to do. They wake up early, they sacrifice themselves, and they live with their goals on replay in their minds. Those who are great at what they do show up early and leave late. They master their craft yet never stop pushing to learn and do more. Don't strive to be average. Don't strive to be good. Instead, strive to be great.

PRACTICE

Greatness is already inside of you, but you have the responsibility of bringing it out. The greats were not great at birth. Those we consider geniuses did not come out the womb with a mastery of their chosen craft. The greats couldn't run, paint, speak, write, or compose as babies. They learned, they found their niche, and then they concentrated on that thing they loved to do. The greats are great because they do a *lot* of what they do. Every day, you should be doing the things at which you want to excel. Seek and discover the intersection of what you like, what you're good at, what you can be paid to do, and then practice. The thing you decide to do with your life, do it a lot. Put in the hours each day. Greatness is not a gene. Greatness is a willingness to push through the pain, frustration, laziness, and inevitable failures that you will face on the road to being great. Greatness takes practice.

BE EFFECTIVE

Being effective does not mean you are busy for the sake of being busy. Being effective means you have a purpose for what you are doing. Effectiveness is the ability to produce a desired result. It means taking action toward the outcome you are longing for. It means having an end goal or result in mind and doing what it takes to cause that desire to become a reality. When you are effective, you are a dream maker. You are a creator. You're able to take an idea, a goal, and a thought, something that once existed only in your imagination and turn it into something tangible. You have the ability to create so create. Don't just be busy. Be effective.

CHOICES

Every second of every day, you're making a choice. Your life is a series of choices, thousands of choices made on a daily basis. Choices are made about what to eat, what to wear, what to do, and how to react to the circumstances you find yourself in moment to moment. With every choice made, consciously or out of habit, you are deciding who you want to be. Out of all the thoughts that run through your head, you choose which ones to focus on. The actions of others directly have an impact on you and on your life, and you choose how to respond to those actions. Your will is your power. Your greatest strength as a human is the ability to make choices about how to spend your energy. Harness that power and utilize that strength. Refuse to be a passive participant in your own life. Do things on purpose and with purpose. Evaluate your habits. Make note of your inputs and how they affect your choices. Be powerful by being in control of your choices.

Do the thing that you love, but also remember to bring love to whatever you do. The majority of your time will not be doing what you love. You will be preparing meals, cleaning, driving, traveling, doing things for other people, or working a job that sustains you while you transition into your dream job. Bring love to all of these things. Bring love into the most tedious and menial tasks. Even if you are among the fortunate who make a living doing what you love, there will be steps in the process that you do not enjoy. Learn to love them. Be patient and kind and don't become frustrated. Be humble in your success and be eager to serve others over yourself. Do not shame yourself or others for their mistakes, but rejoice when things are done right. Persevere until the job is done, no matter what the job is. Bring love to all you do as practice for when you are doing what you truly want to do.

Just do the work. Day after day, do the work. Do the work with love and everything else you want will come. There is no value in chasing money or status. The only value in life is pursuing character. If you are not a person of character, then you won't be able to keep your fortunes when they come. And becoming a person of character comes by doing the work. Faithfulness, integrity, perseverance, patience, self-sacrifice, and discipline are all character traits that will make you a good partner, a good leader, and a good steward. All those traits come from putting in work. Eventually you will have the chance to do the work you were made for, the work that calls to you, but no matter what the work is, just do it. Don't make excuses or become distracted. Focus on the task at hand and do it as best you can. Moment to moment, you must do the work. Day after day, you must do the work. Year after year, you must do the work. There is no way around it. If you want something, work for it!

Inequality in the access to resources and the ability to gain wealth is a reality. You fall somewhere on the spectrum of having a lot or a little. If you are in the majority of the world's population you could probably use more. If you are part of the minority of humans living with more than enough to survive, then it would be of value to share with the majority of people around the world whose quality of life could vastly improve from your generosity. The ambitions to obtain wealth are not bad. Placing the acquisition of wealth at the top of your priority list and selfishly storing riches is. Your life should be spent in the pursuit of happiness for yourself and others, not the pursuit of resources. Consume less and share your excess. You've been taught that sharing is caring before you knew your alphabet, so be generous.

BE CONTENT

You are the source of your happiness. Your attitude makes the call on how content you will be. Only when you decide to be happy for yourself, will you be happy with yourself. When you are content with yourself, then you will be content with all the other things that surround you. Happiness can be elusive. On any given day hundreds of things happen to you that have the potential to rob you of your joy. Don't allow the theft to happen. Let go of worry, bitterness, and anger and find peace of mind. The pursuit of happiness is a pursuit of the mental self-discipline that allows you to seek the good in any circumstance and be content in that circumstance. Your contentment is your choice to make so decide to be content.

LIVE NOW

Your life is meant to be amazing. You are meant to live in abundance and share that abundance with others. You are meant to get the most you can out of life. You have been given specific talents and abilities, and you are supposed to make the most of them. Life will keep going whether you decide to do what you love or not. Time will not stop for you as you try to conquer your fear, but do not let fear stop you. Live the life you want to live. The resources you work hard to gain should empower you to live more, experience more, and see more. Your money shouldn't be hoarded, but invested in your growth and in assisting the growth of others. Be the person you want to be. Take that dance class, learn calligraphy, and pick up that instrument you always wanted to play. Learn that second or third language, ask that crush out, or take a day off to sit in nature. Live your life.

TRUST
YOURSELF

You have more than likely experienced that person who walks into a room and grabs the attention of everyone there. That "it factor," that "x factor," that "swag" is not measurable, but it is real. And the source of this atmosphere-altering phenomenon is self-confidence. Confidence has little to do with personality. The essence of confidence is trust. When you are confident that something will get done, you trust that you or someone else will complete whatever task is presented. Arrogance comes from believing you are better than others, while confidence comes from believing that others can be better by trusting you. Trust that you are uniquely designed to do something and be someone that no one else in the world can do or be. Trusting yourself comes from knowing your value. Knowing your value comes from focusing on the work you have done to get to where you are and believing that you are only getting better. You must think highly of yourself because the world will take you at your own estimate. So dream big, go hard, and trust yourself.

DON'T COMPARE YOURSELF

Comparison is a form of violence against self. To compare yourself to someone else is unproductive and unpleasant. The circumstances that put you in the position you are currently in are yours alone, and they cannot be changed or fully understood by anyone else. The same is true about anyone that you are comparing yourself with. What they had to go through, both internally and externally, to get to where they are now is unknown to you or anyone else. It is much more useful to focus on going after what you want. Being focused on what you don't have only magnifies your problems and minimizes the time you spend focusing on your goals. Every second spent looking at someone else's life is a second spent not focusing on your own mission, so don't waste your time. Celebrate the accomplishments of others, and if you want something similar in your own life, evaluate what you are doing currently. Decide if what you are doing is getting you closer to or further from gaining what you want but don't compare yourself to others.

JUST BE

You live in a beautiful world. Appreciate this planet and all that exists on it. Observe the plants, the ground, and the water. Stop and feel the wind blowing against your skin. Inhale the energy that air provides and feel it recharge your being. Be grateful for all you have and realize that you have far more than you can imagine. Show gratitude in the present while preparing for the future. Be aware of the people you interact with. Give them your attention and focus. Try to learn something new about every person you come in contact with. Don't block out the world around you with technology. Look at what's going on around you. Life in our universe is miraculous and rare. You are among the most blessed beings in existence because you not only have life, but you are also conscious and aware of that life. Embrace that reality. Live in that truth. The present exists, nothing more, nothing less. Accept, appreciate, and learn to love the now. Prepare for the future, but live in the now. Just be.

ABOUT THE AUTHOR

Anthony Chiles has a degree in Civil Engineering from the Missouri University of Science and Technology and currently works as an actor, teacher, and writer. He lives in Los Angeles.

For more info about the author visit: www.anthonychiles.com

ACKNOWLEDGMENTS

Thank you editors Bonnie Sludikoff and Judith Learmann. You make me look like I know what I'm doing. Thanks for getting me in order.

The city of Los Angeles and its people inspire me daily. I'm so glad I moved here. Erick Richardson, thank you for the conversation when you encouraged me to "taste the grits," and make the move from Columbus to Los Angeles. Also, thanks for inspiring the black and white photography.

To all my friends who have enjoyed my Monday Motivation posts over the years, I hope this book helps you when you need to be encouraged.

Years ago my brother gave me the best investment advice ever: invest in yourself. You were so right. The return on my investment has been amazing! I appreciate you being a great example for me from the day I was born. I love you.

My mom and dad are two of the most amazing people I know. Thank you for being, and continuing to be my Monday through Sunday motivation. Without the two of you I would not be the man I am today. No words can express my gratitude for having such awesome people as parents. I love you so much.

I thank the Creator, for making me creative.

~Anthony Chiles

23504364R00064

Made in the USA
San Bernardino, CA
26 January 2019